Yorkshire Dales in Colour

Yorkshire Dales in Colour

Dalesman Books

The Dalesman Publishing Company Ltd.,
Clapham, via Lancaster, LA2 8EB
First Published 1985
© Dalesman Publishing Company Ltd 1985

ISBN: 0 85206 813 1

Printed by Alf Smith & Co., Bradford

Contents

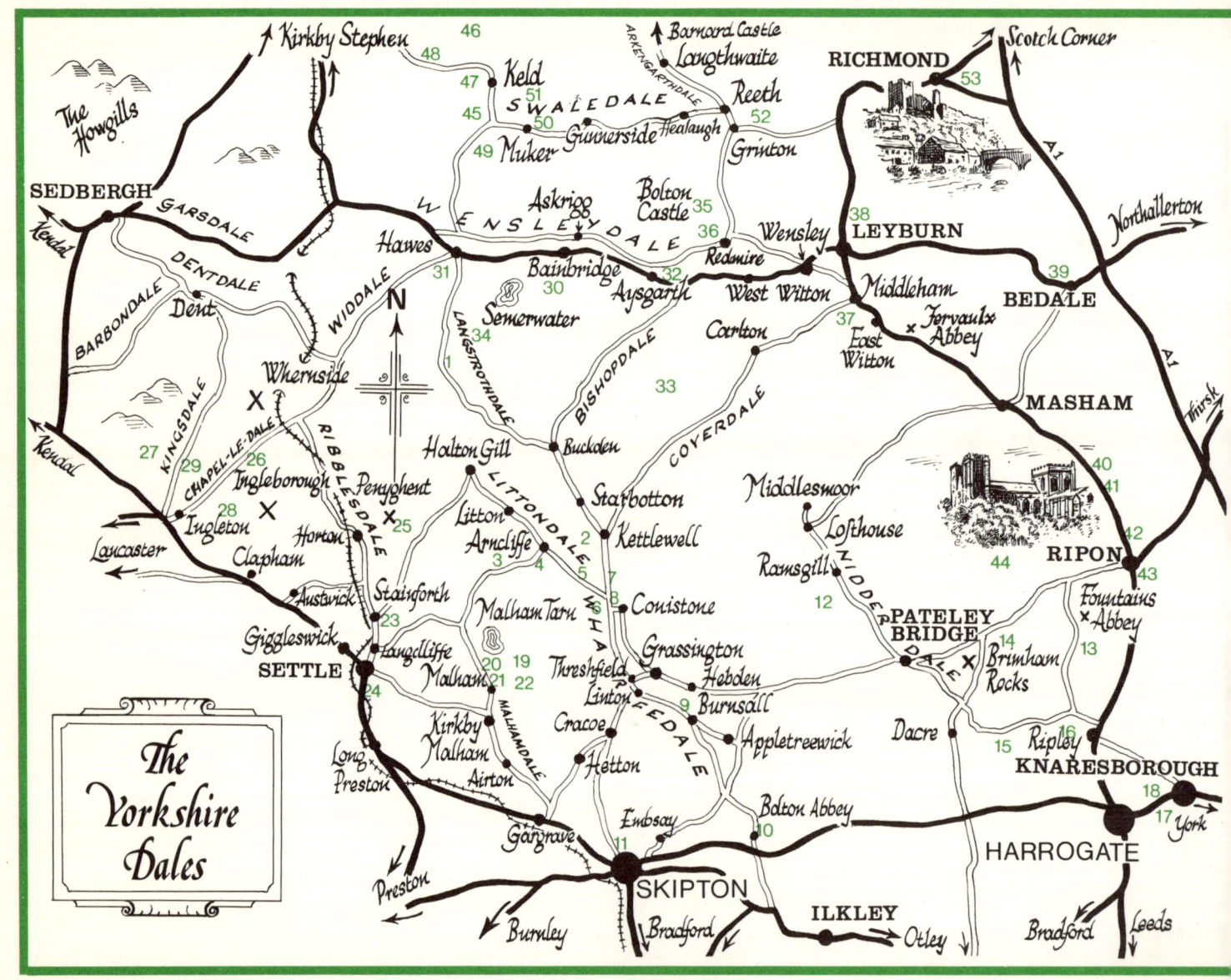

The Yorkshire Dales

The Howgills

Kirkby Stephen   46
48
47   Keld   51   SWALEDALE   Barnard Castle   Langthwaite   RICHMOND   Scotch Corner
45   50   Muker   Gunnerside   Healaugh   Reeth   53
49   Grinton   52
Askrigg   Bolton   Castle   35   Wensley   38   LEYBURN   Northallerton
SEDBERGH   GARSDALE   WENSLEYDALE   36   Redmire   39   BEDALE
Kendal   DENTDALE   Hawes   31   Bainbridge   32   Aysgarth   West Witton   Middleham   Jervaulx   Abbey
BARBONDALE   Dent   WIDDALE   30   Semerwater   34   BISHOPDALE   Carlton   37   East   Witton   MASHAM   Thirsk
1   COVERDALE   33
Whernside   N   Buckden   40   41
27   29   26   Halton Gill   Starbotton   Middlesmoor   Losthouse   42   RIPON
Chapel-le-Dale   Inglebrough   Penyghent   25   Litton   Arncliffe   2   Kettlewell   Ramsgill   44   43
Lancaster   28   Ingleton   Horton   3   4   5   Conistone   12   Fountains   Abbey
Clapham   RIBBLESDALE   7   8   Grassington   PATELEY   BRIDGE   14   Brimham   Rocks   13
Austwick   Stainforth   Malham Tarn   Threshfield   Hebden   Burnsall   Dacre   15   Ripley   16
Giggleswick   Langcliffe   23   20   19   9   Appletreewick   KNARESBOROUGH
SETTLE   24   Malham   21   22   Linton   18
Kirkby   Malham   Cracoe   Hetton   Bolton Abbey   17   York
Long   Preston   Airton   10   HARROGATE
Preston   Gargrave   11   Embsay
SKIPTON   Bradford   Leeds
Burnley   Bradford   ILKLEY   Otley

Key to photographs

Acknowledgements

Jack Kempton: 16, 39, 44
C. R. Kilvington: 20
Tom Nuttall: 36
Tom Parker: 1, 2, 4, 6, 10, 13, 19, 22, 23, 25, 26, 27, 29, 32, 37, 40, 41, 45, 46, 48, 53
Robert Rixon: 9, 31
Clifford Robinson: 7, 14, 18, 43, 49, 50
S. C. Sedgwick: *Front cover* 3, 30, 34, 35
John Smithson: 28
Tony Strong: 15
Christine Whitehead: 52
Derek G. Widdicombe: 42, 47
E. A. Woodall: 11, 17, 24
Malcolm Woods: 8
Geoffrey N. Wright: 5, 12, 21, 33, 38, 51

Maps by J. J. Thomlinson
Drawings by F. Gordon, Janet Rawlins, Herbert Rodmell and J. J. Thomlinson

The Yorkshire Dales

COLOUR gilds the Yorkshire Dales with a thousand shades and hues, each of them fickle, fleeting and ever-changing. They can be seen at their most capricious and exciting at virtually any season of the year except high summer. For then all has gone green — and a dense, dark and all-pervading green at that. There is little to distinguish the overmantle of oozing sycamore leaves from midge-sodden bracken or the mass of silage grass from rain-soaked pasture lands. But come back on an autumn afternoon and the chances are high of being enraptured by an incredible kaleidoscope — a sun-dappled patchwork formed by peat-stained becks, limestone scree, heather-shrouded fells and all the colours of a Dales hillside in the evening of the year. Wander into a wood and let the eyes roam over what at first glance appears to be a gloomy brown carpet of fallen leaves; then look more closely and discover that even here in all this decay is an amazing richness of yellow, orange, ochre and russet, bejeweled by sunrays flickering through mist and the tapestry of branches overhead.

Come the depths of winter and a new dimension is provided by intense low-level light, picking out to superb effect the drystone walls, field patterns and remains of ancient lynchets. Grey and blues predominate, but even in this season of wild weather the palette is enlivened by such dramatic hiccups as the brilliant emerald of sphagnum moss or the occasional creeper-covered cottage. By March the snows are giving way to spring growth, and then suddenly within a matter of weeks the pageant of colour and ever-shifting light returns in even greater glory. Myriads of different greens burst forth in all directions, creating a hauntingly beautiful backcloth for wild violets, Persil-white new-born lambs and golden-yellow daffodils. Camera and canvas struggle to capture the true subtlety of a Dales river in mid-May when the water can be a quite extraordinary shade reflecting tender young foliage on either bank.

The fifty-plus photographs in this book have been selected from views previously published in the pages of *The Dalesman*. They represent fulfilment for a host of photographers, who by a combination of planning, patience and good fortune happened to be in precisely the right place at the right time. Collectively they capture the Dales in many moods and all seasons, and yet among them are some that virtually say it all in one picture.

Take the view of Walden (No. 33), that secluded, little-known valley entered by twin roads sneaking away from the well-manicured village green at West Burton. In the foreground is the inevitable small barn with its two forking holes, one of the most characteristic of Dales features and a relic of the days when almost every meadow had its own laithe for storing winter fodder. Close examination reveals sister structures in many another field. Just visible in the bottom of the valley is a fast-flowing Walden Beck, rushing headlong to join the River Ure, while on either side the irregular pattern of ancient walls gives way to more recent and geometrical moorland enclosures. Purple shadows formed by scudding clouds cast an air of mystery over distant fells. Trees, random planted and once naturally regenerating, add the final touch of Dales perfection to a scene noticeably lacking in human habitation.

Totally dissimilar is the study of Kettlewell from above the Kilnsey road (No. 2) with the Wharfe spanned by a sturdy bridge that bears many a mason's mark. White

Though many places have disappointed me when I have returned to them, the Dales have never disappointed me. I still consider them the finest countryside in Britain, with their magnificent, clean and austere outlines of hill and moor, their charming villages and remote white-washed farms, their astonishing variety of aspect and appeal, from the high gaunt rocks down to the twinkling rivers.

— J. B. Priestley, introducing the first issue of The Dalesman (April 1939)

Of the rural landscapes of England the Yorkshire Dales are to many 'beloved over all'. Where else in England is to be found so large and unspoilt a tract of country with so many high grass-covered hills, so many peopled valleys, so many crystal-clear rivers?

— Marie Hartley & Joan Ingilby, The Yorkshire Dales (1956)

It is a land of pure air, rocky streams and hidden waterfalls. In the winter the roads are often impassable when the heavy snow falls and high fells are a white wilderness where a man could easily lose his way and die. But on summer days when the sun beats down on the lovely miles these uplands are a paradise, the air heavy with the sweetness of warm grass, the breeze carrying a thousand scents from the valley below.

— James Herriot's Yorkshire (1979)

We can create 'new towns', and are doing so, but we cannot create new dales and mountains with their natural beauty and solitude. We must treasure those we have for the deeper spiritual refreshment they can afford to the town-weary majority.

— Arthur Raistrick, The Pennine Dales (1968)

limestone outcrops by the river but it is predominantly grey houses which cluster round Park Gill Beck, grouped so tightly that this might almost be a defensive village shorn of its protecting walls. Cutting diagonally across the picture is the old turbary road, much steeper that it looks, down which in past ages has come ton upon ton of moorland peat for winter fuel. Buttercups in the meadows contrast with harsher greens of high pastures bordering the flanks of Great Whernside, monarch of upper Wharfedale.

Providing yet another distinctive image is Crina Bottom (No. 28), clinging to the rock in the heart of Three Peaks country. Observe the wind-stunted trees, gate-stoops formed from single blocks of gnarled limestone and the cunning way in which past wallers have used a huge boulder to save several feet of hard endeavour. Although in a valley, this remote farmhouse is almost twelve hundred feet above sea level, almost the same height that separates it from the summit of Ingleborough whose brooding presence here is for ever felt.

Utterly different in character, these three photographs were all taken within two dozen miles of each other. Nowhere else in the world can offer such incredible variety in so small a space; herein lies the true magic of the Yorkshire Dales. To visit them but once is to know them not: it takes half a lifetime just to explore this region of constant surprise and delight, and another half to claim full knowledge and understanding.

The constant succession of deep valleys and high fells makes the area seem much larger than is really the case — both vertically and horizontally. Modest hills look like majestic peaks, especially when clothed in snow, and in the rainy season small becks have all the power of mighty rivers. Natives of Wharfedale see Swaledale as another country, worlds away as a result of high passes which in winter often become blocked and compel enormous detours. Fell tops, where the sound of silence is broken only by bleating sheep, the cries of moorland birds and — horrors! — low-flying jet aircraft, are different in every way to the valley bottoms where farm and village life pursues its measured pace. Each major dale has its own individuality, and so too does each tributary valley. Apedale, Crummackdale, Cotterdale and Gunnerside Gill are but four of many a score, a fact that alone makes the Dales so difficult to know intimately.

Everwhere there is variety. Explore the broad green floor of Wensleydale and then the U-shaped confines of Littondale. Revel in the near-limitless panorama down Bishopdale from Kidstones Pass before peering into the dingy depths of Yew Cogar Scar from above Arncliffe. Gasp at the sight of Aysgarth Falls in spate — a spectacle preferred by some early travellers to the cataracts of the Nile; stare awestruck at Hardrow Force as it drops almost a hundred feet from its deeply undercut lip; or poise cautiously on slippery rocks beside the Strid and watch the Wharfe in turmoil as it is forced through a channel only a few feet wide. Gaze up at the mountains and realise instantly that the 'crouching lion' of Penyghent and 'sleeping elephants' of the Howgills have nothing in commom. Pay homage to epic Malham Cove, highspot of limestone country, and imagine the Dales can offer no equal; then discover that wind-battered Brimham Rocks provide grandeur of another shade in the gritstone region.

Even if you visit the same place or make the same journey time after time, the sense of wonderment is still sustained. Pennine weather, which offers everything from torrential rain blown upwards in the teeth of a gale to scorching summer days under a lazy azure sky, ensures that the ever-essential light and colour are seldom similar. Ingleborough from the top of Fleet Moss on a winter afternoon with, if the luck prevails, a glimpse of the sun setting over far-away Morecambe Bay, is a very different

Wensleydale near Hawes

vision to the same scene on an autumn morning when mist can fill the valleys and make upper Ribblesdale look like a great grey sea with the peaks protruding as barren islands.

The man-made landscape provides yet more departures from dull uniformity. Wensleydale villages such as Castle Bolton or East Witton, with their cottages staring at each other across a broad green, are far removed from the huddle of houses seen at Starbotton or Thwaite. Even the place-names have their own music — where else could you find them tripping off the tongue so pleasurably as do Arkleside, Booze, Cosh, Drebley, Egglestone, Feizor and Giggleswick? Each major dale has its own gateway town, and again no two are alike. Skipton has its splendid High Street bounded by parish church at one end and Woolworths at the other; Settle nestles under the great rock of

Castlebergh and with dwellings such as The Folly and The Shambles might almost be thought to have an inferiority complex; Knaresborough rises precipitously from the banks of a River Nidd placid enough to permit pleasure-boating; Ripon is a pocket-sized cathedral city with traditions dating back a thousand years; and Richmond with its Georgian theatre and vast market place for ever cherishes the memory of its 'sweet lass'.

Individual buildings tell a similar story. The traditional houses of Wharfedale have a conscious element of display not found in the northern dales, while chimney pots, porches, windows and fireplaces come in a hundred and more varieties. Barns range from double-doored structures, often more imposing than the adjoining farm dwelling, to the tiny hovels that dot the hillsides of upper Swaledale. Churches descend from the sublime as seen at

A Poem from the Dales

Song of Kettlewell
by Halliwell Sutcliffe

Oh, would ye seek for ease of heart,
Ye wayfarers so sad?
Then fare away from street and mart,
And hear the streams be glad.

Oh, would ye seek for peace of soul,
Ye street-bound, hapless folk?
Then make the cleanly North your goal—
'Twill ease you from the yoke.

Oh, would ye rest awhile and dream,
Ye hurrying slaves of life?
Then seek the ways of Wharfe's brown stream
And meads where pace is rife.

Oh, would ye know good human cheer,
Ye men who lack the faith?
Then roam where God and sky are near
And unbelief's a wraith.

Oh, would ye find your ease of heart,
Ye heart-sore kin of mine?
Then choose the simple, better part
And drink the good North Wine.

Oh, would ye walk with peace for wife,
Ye wifeless, weary wights?
Then walk where there is cease of strife,
Save of the wind o'nights.

Oh, would ye find a garden fair,
Ye bondsmen of the street?
Then seek my dainty village, where
The Heartsease Maidens meet.

Oh, would ye bless a comrade guide,
Ye lost folk in the rain?
Then speed to Kettlewell the Bride
And find your faith again.

Hubberholme, Grinton and Kirkby Malham to plain 19th century edifices flung up when many Dales villages suffered almost uncontrollable expansion during a boom in the lead-mining industry. Bridges could fill a book in their own right, and even the drystone walls with their stiles and hog-holes display many a local trait.

How, then, is the unique variety and mystique of the Dales surviving in an age where conformity and mediocrity are increasingly the norm? All the photographs in this book are relatively recent and yet, take away the odd car or double-yellow line, and most of them could have been taken quarter of a century or more ago. Change is coming to the Dales but it is not all-pervading.

An era of increased mobility that began with the railways and continued with the invention of the internal combustion engine has culminated in a situation in which eight million people now live within 1½ hours' travelling time of Skipton. The result has been an incessant demand for weekend cottages and holiday accommodation, forcing prices up to a level that has driven out the so-called locals and left many villages in the higher Dales denuded of life in the winter months. Calls for more intensive agricultural production, coupled with availability of materials far cheaper and easier to handle than native stone and timber, have seen the familiar field barn ousted in favour of massive prefabricated structures quite out of tone and scale with the average Dales community. Their predecessors have either been converted into second homes or left to fall into ruin. The memory that many visitors must now take away with them is the all-pervading stink of silage, rapidly taking over from hay as the commonest form of winter feed. In the area of mineral extraction, the once small quarries in the limestone regions have grown at a prodigious rate which might have been more acceptable if the exceptionally pure stone had been used for high-grade chemical purposes rather than merely squandered as aggregate in road-building schemes.

Yet despite all these assaults, the Dales have somehow survived. Perhaps in part it has just been a matter of good luck — a guardian angel hovering somewhere in the remote fastnesses of back-of-beyond Arkengarthdale. A main line railway from Liverpool to Newcastle was almost thrust through Wharfedale and Bishopdale in the 1840s, although even here one cannot overlook the praise now being heaped on that later intrusion into Three Peaks country — the Settle to Carlisle line — whose pending doom is vehemently opposed by conservationists far and wide. When Bradford's thirst for water assumed insatiable proportions at the end of the Victorian era, the city first considered flooding Burnsall by building an enormous dam just south of the village. Second choice fell on upper Nidderdale, where three huge reservoirs created what is often termed 'Yorkshire's Little Switzerland'.

Such recurring threats increased pressure from dales lovers if not dalesmen for the 1954 creation of the Yorkshire Dales National Park, an institution often maligned, frequently misunderstood and inevitably more villified for its failures than praised for its undoubted successes. With its powers in reality extremely limited, the problems have only multiplied — yet in so many cases the worst fears have somehow not quite been realised. Centuries of decline of natural woodland have been controversially reversed by planting regimented masses of Sitka spruce, although not as the foresters once hoped in the heart of the Three Peaks. The Dales — always a walker's paradise — have in parts become over-trodden, but even so footpath erosion is not on the scale of the Peak District and it is still possible to spend a whole day in less frequented haunts without seeing another living soul. There are no all-conquering highways such as have despoiled the Lake District, no large hotels or chair lifts to select vantage

Wainwath Falls, upper Swaledale

points. Momentary panic ensued when it looked as if Ingleborough's summit plateau had been chosen as the perfect sight for an early warning station, but then it was noticed that the plans bore the same date as April Fool's Day!

The Dales have had few heroes and even fewer aristocrats — dalesfolk, more at home dealing with sheep than snobbery, have never suffered ostentatiousness gladly. Yet here and there the odd honeypot such as the Bolton Abbey estate, creation of successive Dukes of Devonshire, helps to siphon off untold numbers of day visitors and thus ease pressure on the more vulnerable heartland. There is no equivalent of Wordworth's Dove Cottage or even the Brontes' Wuthering Heights, although James Herriot has achieved in a few short years of television exposure what the various tourist agencies failed to accomplish in a decade of hard-sought publicity. Suddenly the area has become a media-man's delight, the setting for a whole gamut of plays, films and documentaries as producers and directors discover that here in the unpromising 1980s is a part of England where time has been kind to both characters and their country — this land of fickle light and fleeting colour. The magic of the Yorkshire Dales still remains.

— **David Joy**
February 1985

Limestone pavement near Ingleborough

Wharfedale

1. River Wharfe near Beckermonds

2. Kettlewell

Main centre for the higher dale, Kettlewell still has three inns — a reminder of the days when it was an important stopping point on the old coaching road over Park Rash to Richmond. The weathered stone bridge which takes the main road over the Wharfe boasts a wealth of masons' marks. Behind the village, green pastures give way to rolling moorland and the 2,310 ft. summit of Great Whernside.

3. Littondale from above Arncliffe

Miles of limestone walls and much ancient woodland cannot disguise the classic glacial U-shape of Littondale. It takes its name not from its river — the Skirfare — but from the village of Litton; anciently the valley was known as Amerdale.

4. Arncliffe village

Today the main settlement in Littondale is Arncliffe, where the houses cluster round a large village green carpeted with yellow coltsfoot in season. It was here that Charles Kingsley wrote part of 'The Water Babies' whilst staying at Bridge End, a 17th century house beside the Skirfare.

5. Hawkswick

Missed by many a traveller, this comely village lies on the minor road along the east side of Littondale. It probably takes its name from the hawks that used to nest on the steep limestone scars sheltering the houses from the north-east winds.

It is a matter of wonder to me that, with such a spring, the beautiful scenery of the neighbourhood, its healthy atmosphere, and many other admirable, interesting, and important features, Kilnsey has not become before now an established resort of invalids. Persons of imagination and capital might make it a powerful rival of Ilkley . . . Indeed, I begin, while standing here, to see in imagination the village enlarged almost beyond recognition. I see new streets of houses, splendid hotels for visitors, and gentlemen's mansions to which are attached tastefully laid out grounds. I behold all kinds of conveyances, from the common cart to the nobleman's carriage, full of pleasure-seekers hurrying in different directions.

– B. J. Harker, 'Rambles in Upper Wharfedale' (1869)

6. Kilnsey Crag

Jutting out into the valley like a stranded sea cliff, Kilnsey's Sphinx-like headland towers 170 feet above the valley floor. Its remarkable 40 feet overhang at the top is a creation of the last Ice Age. As so often in the Dales, daffodils bloom while pockets of snow still cling to distant peaks.

7 & 8.   Kilnsey Show

Held in the shadow of Kilnsey's lowering crag, the now almost over-popular Upper Wharfedale Agricultural Show takes place on Summer Bank Holiday Tuesday. Town and country rub shoulders, watching the fell race or the parade of heavy horses while the children munch ice creams or stroke the back of a hopefully well-tethered bull. Kilnsey must boast some of the best drystone walls in the Dales — the product of one of the most fascinating competitions at the show.

The chief glory of Burnsall is the river, and the bridge which crosses it is the successor of many flood-tormented earlier structures. When Burnsall Bridge was restored in 1612 the bill was met by Sir William Craven, the 'Dick Whittington of the Dales' who was born in a poor home at nearby Appletreewick, journeyed to London to seek his fortune and eventually became Lord Mayor of the City. The tiny village green beside the Wharfe is the setting on 'the first Saturday after the first Sunday after August 12th' for Burnsall Feast Sports, an event dating back to Elizabethan times. Its highlight is the Classic Fell Race, involving runners in a climb of almost a thousand feet.

9.   Burnsall Bridge

The glories of Bolton are on the north; for there, whatever the most fastidious taste could require to constitute a perfect landscape is not only found, but in its proper place. In front, and immediately under the eye, lies a smooth expanse of park-like enclosure, spotted with native elm, ash, &c, of the finest growth; on the right, an oak wood, with jutting points of grey rock; on the left a rising copse. Still forward are seen the aged groves of Bolton Park, the growth of centuries; and farther yet, the barren and rocky distances of Simon Seat and Barden Fell, contrasted to the warmth, fertility, and luxuriant foliage of the valley below.

– T. D. Whitaker, 'History of Craven', (1805)

10.   River Wharfe at Bolton Abbey

11.   Skipton — Gateway to the Dales

The most memorable feature of this bustling town is the High Street, flanked by trees and stone setts and dominated at its northern end by the parish church. Perpendicular in style, the church contains some remarkable monuments to the Clifford family whose impressive castle is entered through a gateway just off the Bolton Abbey road.

Nidderdale

12. Nidderdale from above Wath

Some ten miles east of Nidderdale, the best preserved of all abbeys in England is at the same time the finest of picturesque ruins. Fountains owes the magnificence of its setting to William Aislabie's vision in linking its grounds with those of his country seat at Studley Royal, thus creating a stupendous landscape garden. By far and away the most impressive approach to Fountains is through Studley Park, with its avenues of trees, the river, temples, statues, lakes — and a herd of fallow and red deer. The property is now in the care of the National Trust.

13.   Fountains Abbey

14. Brimham Rocks

Perched almost a thousand feet above sea level on the eastern flanks of Nidderdale, Brimham Rocks represent perhaps the best example in Britain of wind-erosion in desert conditions. They were produced in late Carboniferous times when heavy masses of millstone grit were lifted to the surface by pressures from beneath. Heat, frost and moisture gradually shattered the particles of rock which were blown against the faces and bases of the gritstone masses to create the strangely sculptured shapes that today give the moor such an air of mystery. The National Trust now look after what is claimed to be 'the world's most interesting collection of rocks'.

Up dale to Angram, everything had gone smoothly. The walk from Harrogate by way of Hampsthwaite, Birstwith and Darley had been without incident other than the pleasure of renewing old memories of that delightful country and of feeling again the thrill of surprise as I climbed up to Darley and saw half Nidderdale at my feet . . . As I crossed the bridge at dusk, the moon came up and the sky filled with stars. The little chain of villages that lie between Dacre and Pateley – Summer Bridge, Smelt Houses, Wilsill and Glasshouses – took on a ghostly solemnity as I strode past, and, deep below, the Nidd flowed silver under the moon.

– Alfred J. Brown, 'Broad Acres' (1948)

15. Autumn at Hampsthwaite

16. Ripley

The market cross is one of the few ancient features of Ripley, for in 1827-8 the whole place was rebuilt in the style of a typical French village in Alsace Lorraine. Responsible for this whimsicle creation was Sir William Amcotts Ingilby of Ripley Castle — seat of the Ingilby family for 600 years.

Knaresborough, among the Dales' market-towns, has a place all its own. In situation and character it is like some pleasant foreigner come to settle in the North. Its colour is not made up of greys and lichen-greens – as Skipton's is, and Settle's, and many other town's. Its tiled roofs somehow give the place its subtle air of warmth and well-being. They have mellowed into shades of mulberry and brown and ochre that blend in unobtrusive harmony. Nidd, brown and tranquil, washes Knaresborough's feet . . . The irises thrive here, and paeonies, and lavender walks. On summer evenings, when the dusk is warm and still, you ask for the nightingale and wonder that he dare not roam into our northern country.

– Halliwell Sutcliffe, 'The Striding Dales'
(1930)

17. Knaresborough

One of the oldest and most beautiful of inland resorts, Knaresborough marks the point where Nidderdale has a final burst of epic scenery before dissolving into the Vale of York. Woods, parkland, ruined castle, old church, and the gorge with the river winding below ancient cottages are just some of its many charms. The castellated viaduct has been described as 'one of the most notable railway crimes of England'.

18. Knaresborough Market

Malhamdale

19. Entrance to Gordale Scar

In Malham Cove the stones of the brook were softer with moss than any silken pillow; the crowded oxalis-leaves yielded to the pressure of the hand, and were not felt; the cloven leaves of the herb-robert and robed clusters of its companion overflowed every rent in the rude crags with living balm; there was scarcely a place left by the tenderness of happy things where one might not lay down one's forehead on their warm softness and sleep.

– John Ruskin, 'Proserpina'

20 & 21. Malham Cove

One of the great glories of the Dales, Malham Cove is a natural amphitheatre of dazzling white limestone more than 300 feet high and 300 yards long. Bubbling into daylight at the foot of the cliff is Malham Beck — not, as is often supposed, the River Aire which rises to the south of Malham Village. The Cove is one of the highspots of the Pennine Way, back-packers often pausing on the limestone pavement at the top to enjoy the view and contemplate the many miles of hard slog ahead.

22.   Road to Gordale Scar

Purple flowers of roadside cranesbill
provide the only contrast in an
otherwise green and white landscape
on the narrow road from Malham village
to Gordale. From this distance the Scar
looks quite ordinary, its true
magnificence only being revealed
when one leaves the road and
suddenly enters a vast gorge, 400 feet
deep, down which Gordale Beck
rushes in two great leaps.

Ribblesdale
and the Three Peaks Country

23.   **Ribblesdale panorama from above Langcliffe**

24. Settle Market

At 2,273 ft. Penyghent is the lowest but by no means the least spectacular of Yorkshire's famed Three Peaks. Its name means 'Hill of the Winds' and in shape it has been likened to a crouching lion. Penyghent catches the wind and seems to retain snow longer than the other great summits; snow has been known to drift to depths of 30 feet leaving traces as late in the year as June. Superb views of the peak are obtained from the road over from Stainforth past Rainscar to Halton Gill.

25.   Penyghent from Rainscar

Flat-topped Ingleborough is undoubtedly the most popular of the Three Peaks. Its distinctive shape dominates the surrounding country for miles around and looms large from closer viewpoints such as Kingsdale (right) and Crina Bottom (far right). The large, windswept plateau of the 2,373 ft. peak was in part shaped by Brigantean tribesfolk who encircled their horseshoe-shaped huts with a 3,000 ft. stone rampart and used this impregnable position for defence.

26. Limestone pavement near Ingleborough

27 & 28.   Ingleborough — Yorkshire's most distinctive mountain

29. Thornton Force

Ancient pre-Cambrian rocks are
conspicuous in the area around the
Force, a highlight of the Falls Walk from
Ingleton through the glens of Doe and
Twiss. Paths and bridges were built a
century ago to make these little valleys
accessible on a tour of some 4¼ miles.

Wensleydale

30.   Bainbridge village green

Hawes, capital of upper Wensleydale, derives its name from the Anglo-Saxon 'haus' meaning a mountain pass. It claims to be the highest market town in England — although so do Princetown on Dartmoor and Alston in Cumbria! On market day, Tuesday, the whole town has a carnival atmosphere with farming families from places round about joining the local folk.

31.   Market Day at Hawes

32. River Ure cascading over Aysgarth High Force

33 & 34.   Two 'little dales' — Walden and Raydale

One of the smallest of cities, Ripon slopes down to the Ure and forms an imposing gateway to Wensleydale. The market cross, a mighty obelisk some ninety feet high, is from the end of the 18th century and is surmounted by ornamental ironwork and a guilded horn as a weathervane. Nearby is the town hall designed by James Wyatt, with the pediment of its front supported by four columns and a cornice on which in letters of gold are the words, 'Except the Lord keep the city the Wakeman waketh in vain' — a reference to a custom dating back more than a thousand years.

42. Ripon Market

Among the most endearing features of the Yorkshire Dales are the scores of minor tributary valleys, many of them never discovered by the tourist in a hurry. Wensleydale is especially rich in such gems. Walden (far left) is a six-mile long valley reached by two cul-de-sac roads which leave the top end of the green in the attractive village of West Burton. Raydale, south of Bainbridge, is best known for Semerwater — Yorkshire's third largest inland lake after Hornsea Mere and Malham Tarn. The outflow from the lake forms the River Bain, only three miles long and claiming to be the shortest river in England.

For five and a half centuries and more Bolton Castle has stood, a cidadel, on thc slopes of Wensleydale. For more than half that time it was a citadel in fact as well as name, guarding the dales folk against marauding Scots, playing its part in the turbulent politics of the age, serving as a prison for Mary of Scotland. The Civil War put an end to its active life, and ever since it has stood, a ruin, dominating the landscape of the dale – dreaming, perhaps, of past splendours.

– Lord Bolton, Foreword to 'Bolton Castle' by George Jackson (1946)

35. Bolton Castle

36. Redmire

Shaded by a sycamore tree, the old cross with a new pillar dominates one of several small greens that are a feature of Redmire. The village stares out across one of Wensleydale's well-wooded reaches to distant Penhill.

37.   East Witton

Cherry blossom time brings extra glory to East Witton — a village already more than merely attractive with its two main rows of houses, each connected by shallow steps, alongside a broad tract of grass. It lies between Leyburn and Middleham.

38. Leyburn Market

Thus wandering we reach Bedale, a clean little town, still having that appearance of dream and slumber peculiar to ancient towns with comfortable inns, a charming little river flowing through meadows, in fact, just the place for peace-loving people to spend their days. Yet to-day is the one busy day of the week . . . around the market cross a motley crowd assembles, and all are busily engaged in bustle, chaffing, and bargaining. Market baskets and hampers, from which peep heads and necks of ducks, hens and cockerels; smaller baskets contain bantams, doves, etc. On the stalls are eggs, butter, cheese, apples, plums, and vegetables, and even a stall with an array of cheap ribbons, and other riff raff.

– Edmund Bogg, 'From Edenvale to the Plains of York'

39. Bedale Market

Midway between Masham and Ripon, West Tanfield is a photographer's dream with the now placid Ure flowing past well-groomed gardens and under an old three-arched bridge. Grouped nearby are the church, the lovely Chantry Cottage and the Marmion Tower, a 15th century gatehouse with its intriguing window above the great arch. The tombs of the Marmions, a family who came here as long ago as 1215, are to be seen inside the church which has woodwork by Robert Thompson, the 'mouseman' of Kilburn.

40 & 41.   West Tanfield

Ripon is a town that cherishes its tradition. At nine o'clock every evening a horn-blower, wearing a three-cornered hat, blows the Wakeman's Horn at the mayor's house and at the market cross. The custom goes back to the reign of Elizabeth, when the town was governed by a wakeman and an alderman. To escape robbery, every householder paid a small fee to the wakeman, whose business it was to set a watch and to be responsible for the safety of the town until the horn was blown again at sunrise. If a robber did break into a house and take anything the wakeman had to repay the householder for the loss.

– Lettice Cooper, 'Yorkshire – West Riding' (1950)

43. The Hornblower at Ripon

44. Ripon Cathedral

Ripon actually lies on the tiny River Skell, whose waters flow close to one of England's smallest cathedrals — only 270 feet long but 87 feet wide. Its greatest treasure is the Saxon crypt, built by St. Wilfrid in about 669.

Swaledale

45.   Winter in upper Swaledale near Keld

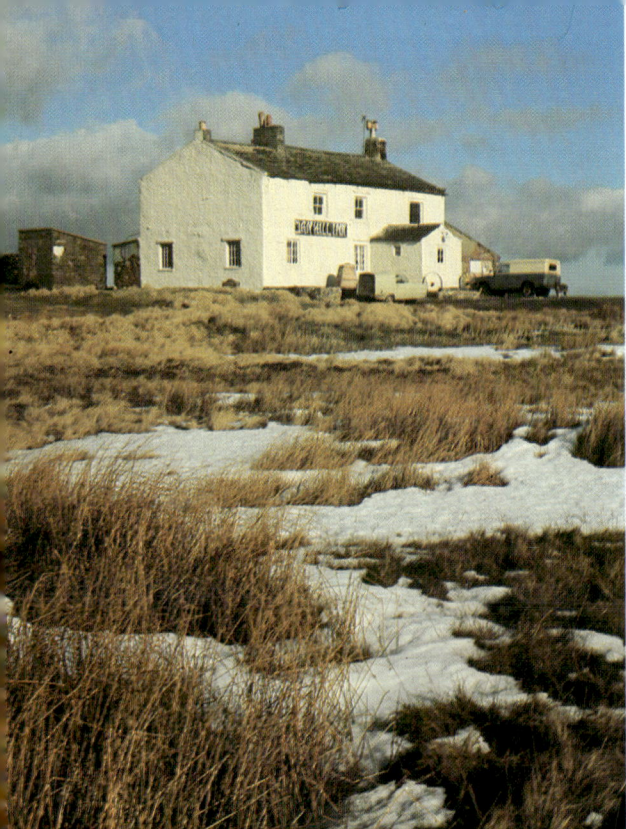

Swaledale's upper reaches have their own irresistible magic, due partly to the sense of remoteness and partly to the sheer beauty of this wild yet secluded countryside. Follow the road that climbs up through West Stonesdale to Tan Hill — at 1,732 ft. the highest inn in England — and you look out over a vast area of moorland that seems to stretch to illimitable horizons. Down below, the Swale begins with the merging of Great Sleddale and Birkdale becks and soon flows over a succession of waterfalls that create a feeling of sustained excitement.

47. River Swale near Keld

46. Tan Hill Inn

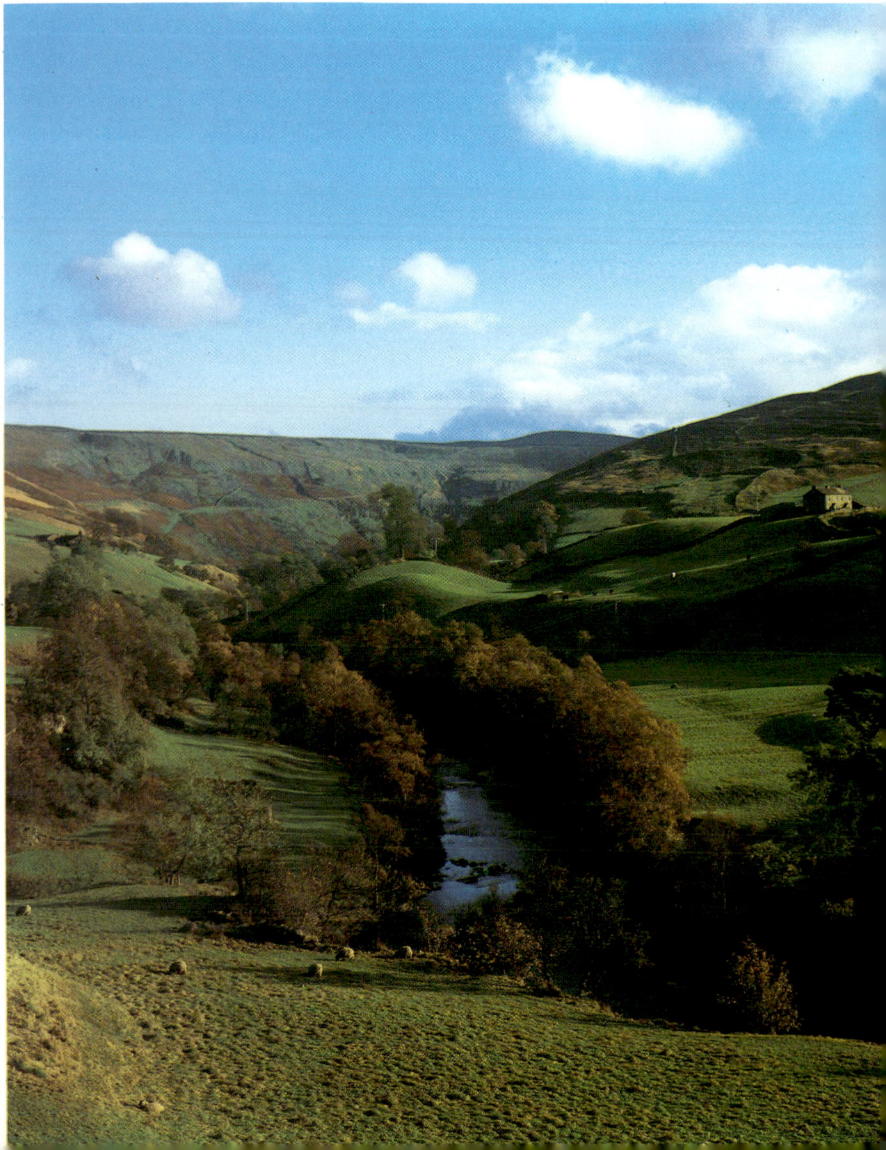

The little cluster of stone buildings at Keld, haphazardly yet tidily arranged, is attractively situated on a headland above the Swale. Little has changed here for generations past, and proud dates and names of proud men adorn the doorways and walls and even the chapel belfry: a sundial records the hours but time here is measured in centuries. Keld is the end of Swaledale; beyond are the wild moors of the watershed. Cottages, chapels and the many many barns stand starkly against a barren background, but the joy of Keld is the swift-flowing river, embowered in trees, sheltered by white cliffs of limestone, and broken by falls and cataracts on its helter-skelter course from the bleak hills to the gentler pastures of the valley. Always, at Keld, there is the sound of the river.

   – A. Wainwright, 'Pennine Way Companion'

48. Wainwath Falls

One of the best-known villages in Swaledale, Muker nestles close to the foot of the once infamous Buttertubs Pass which in almost Alpine-like style offers a direct link with Hawes. Muker stands on a small beck and not the Swale as many visitors suppose. The river flows behind Kisdon Hill, over which runs the old Corpse Road — so named from the days when the bodies of those who died were conveyed on foot to Grinton church.

49 & 50. Muker village

All the Yorkshire dales convey a totally different impression when viewed from on high, and especially so Swaledale which is both deep and narrow. This, coupled with the fact that the valley runs east-west, creates one of the dale's few drawbacks, for in winter many of the villages scarcely see the sun between November and February. Shivering shady days are soon forgotten in the summer months when all has gone green, or even in the depths of winter down-dale at Reeth where the broader landscape glistens crispy white in fleeting shafts of sunlight.

51. Muker from the Kisdon road

52. Reeth from
Fremington Edge

53.   The Keep, Richmond Castle

Six Dales in Pictorial Maps

The numbers at the bottom of each map correspond with the illustration numbers in this book.

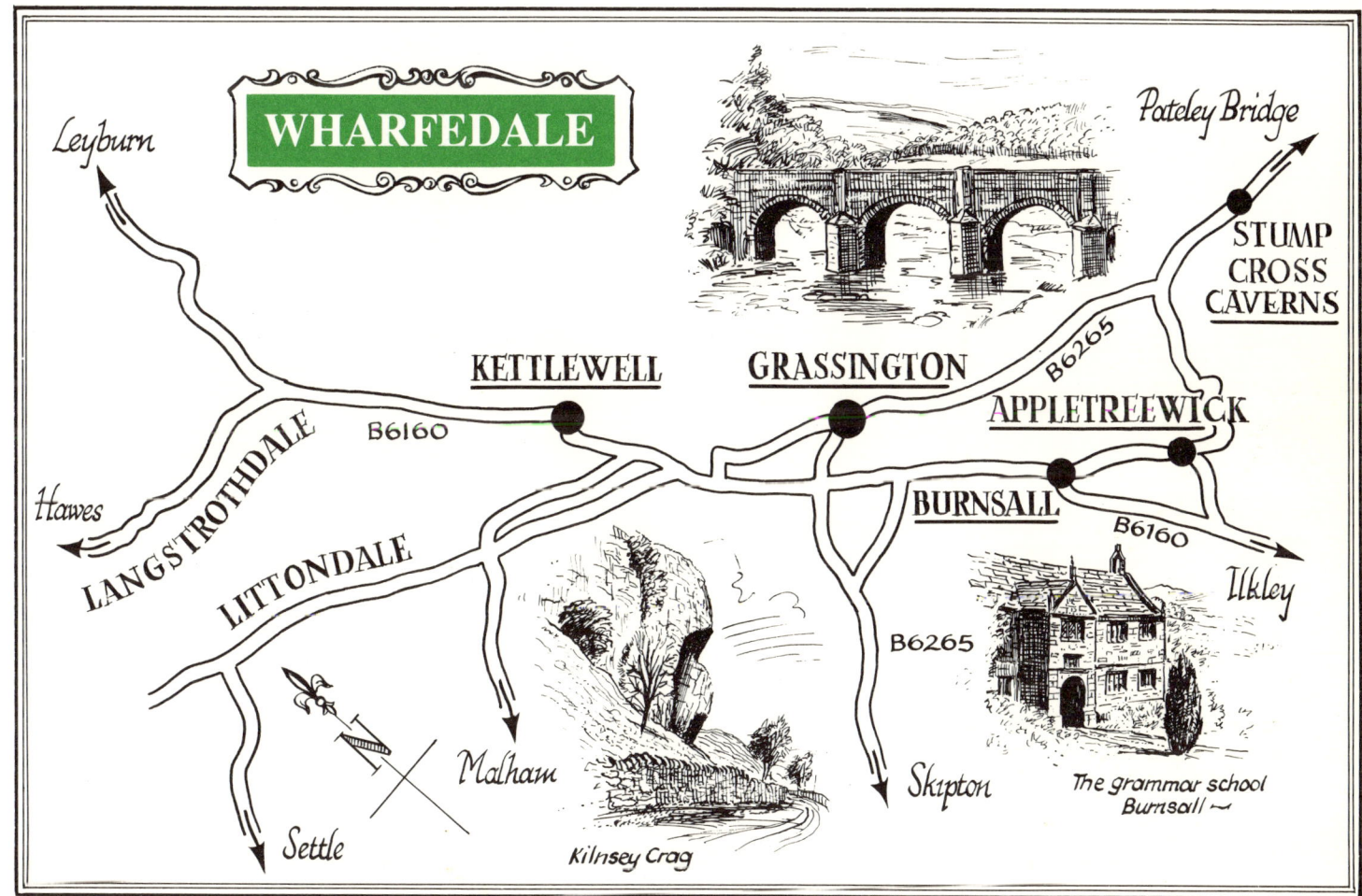

WHARFEDALE

Leyburn

Pateley Bridge

STUMP CROSS CAVERNS

Hawes

LANGSTROTHDALE

LITTONDALE

B6160

KETTLEWELL

GRASSINGTON

B6265

APPLETREEWICK

BURNSALL

B6160

Ilkley

B6265

Malham

Settle

Kilnsey Crag

Skipton

The grammar school
Burnsall ~

1 — 10

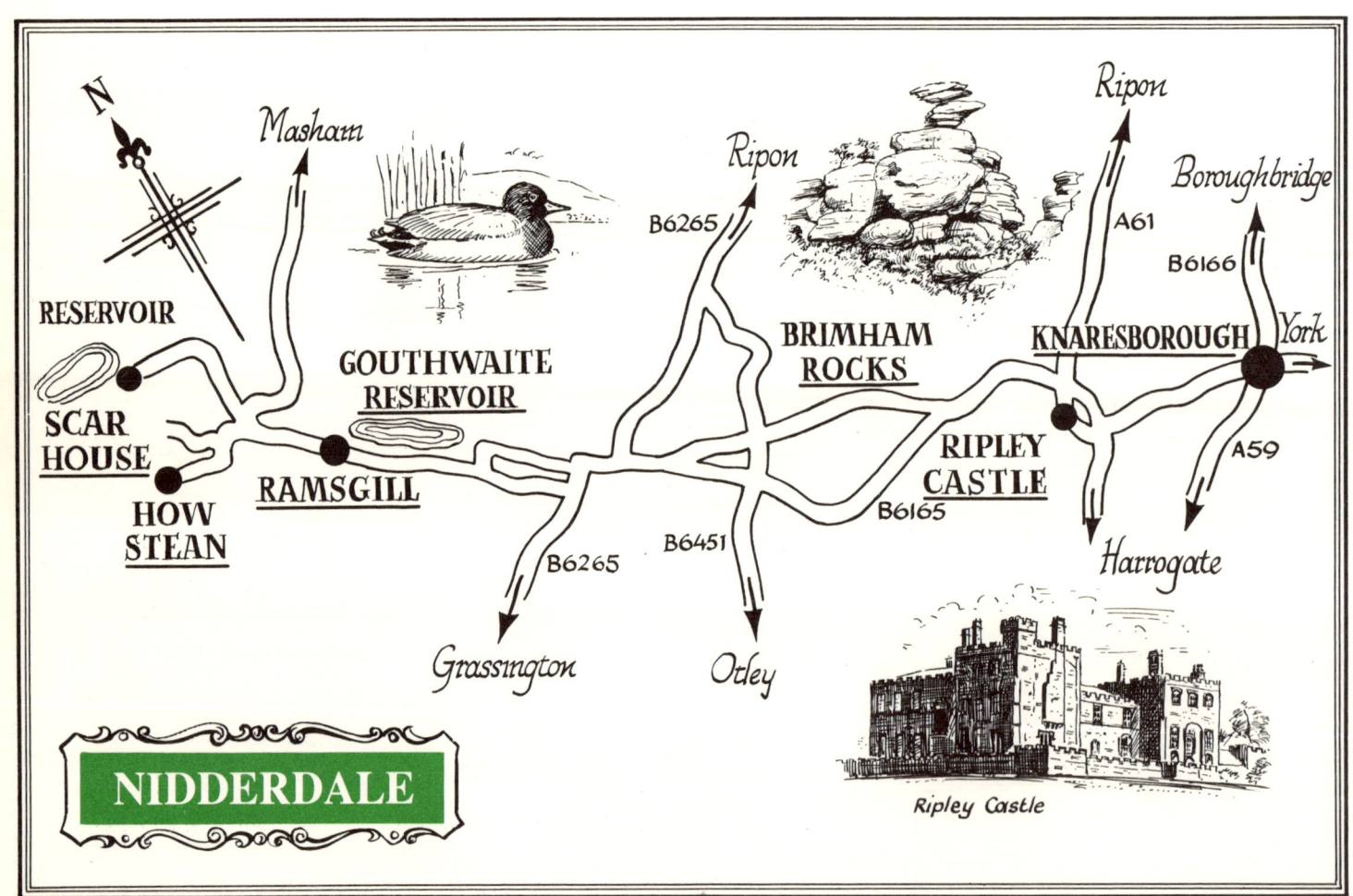

N

Masham

RESERVOIR

SCAR
HOUSE

HOW
STEAN

RAMSGILL

GOUTHWAITE
RESERVOIR

B6265

Ripon

B6265

B6451

Grassington

Otley

BRIMHAM
ROCKS

RIPLEY
CASTLE

B6165

Ripon

A61

Boroughbridge

B6166

KNARESBOROUGH   *York*

Harrogate

A59

Ripley Castle

NIDDERDALE

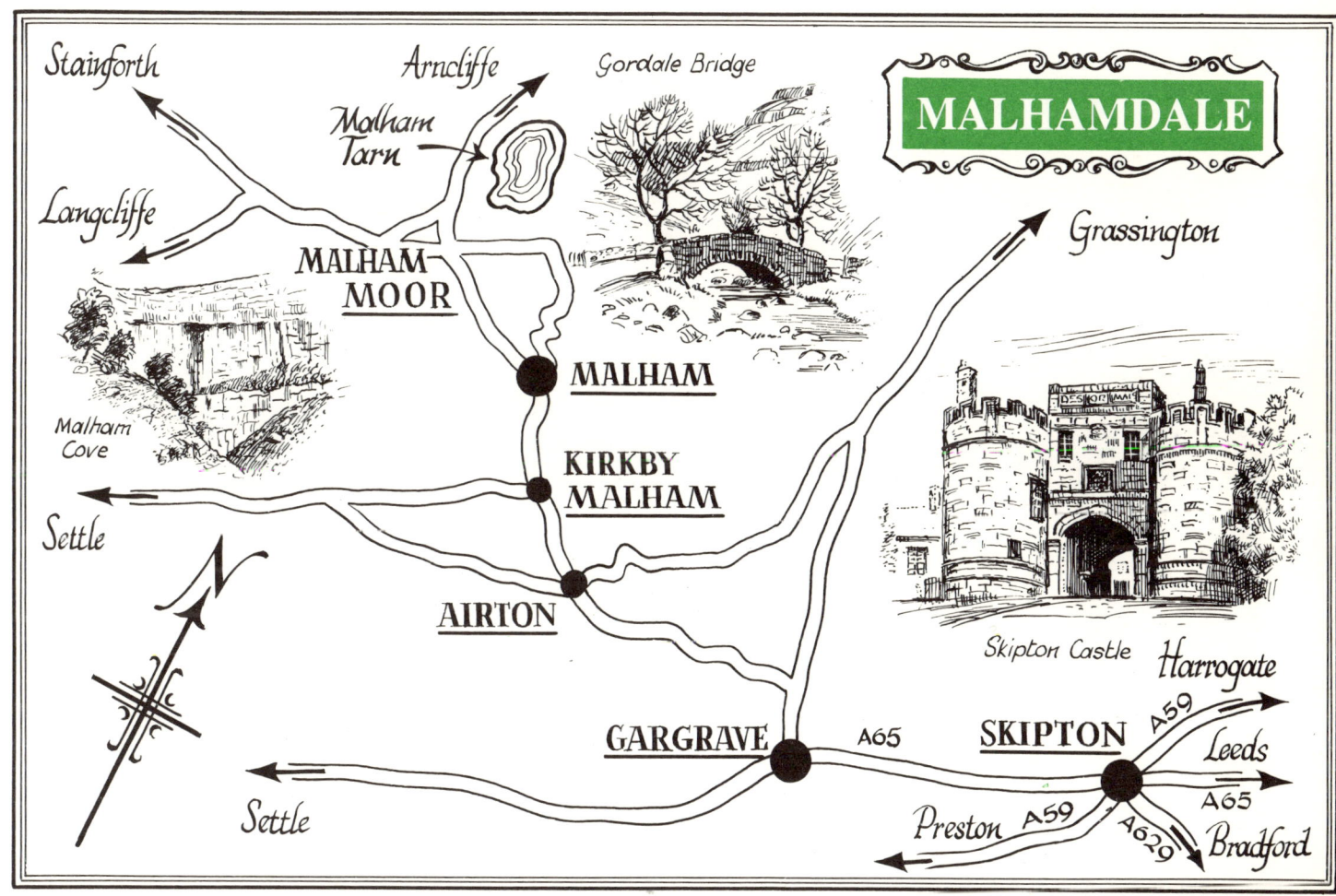

Stainforth

Arncliffe

Gordale Bridge

MALHAMDALE

Malham
Tarn

Langcliffe

**MALHAM
MOOR**

● **MALHAM**

Malham
Cove

Grassington

● **KIRKBY
MALHAM**

Settle

N

● **AIRTON**

Skipton Castle

Harrogate

GARGRAVE ●

A65

SKIPTON ●

A59

Settle

Preston A59

A629

Leeds

A65

Bradford

RIBBLESDALE and the Three Peaks

23 — 29

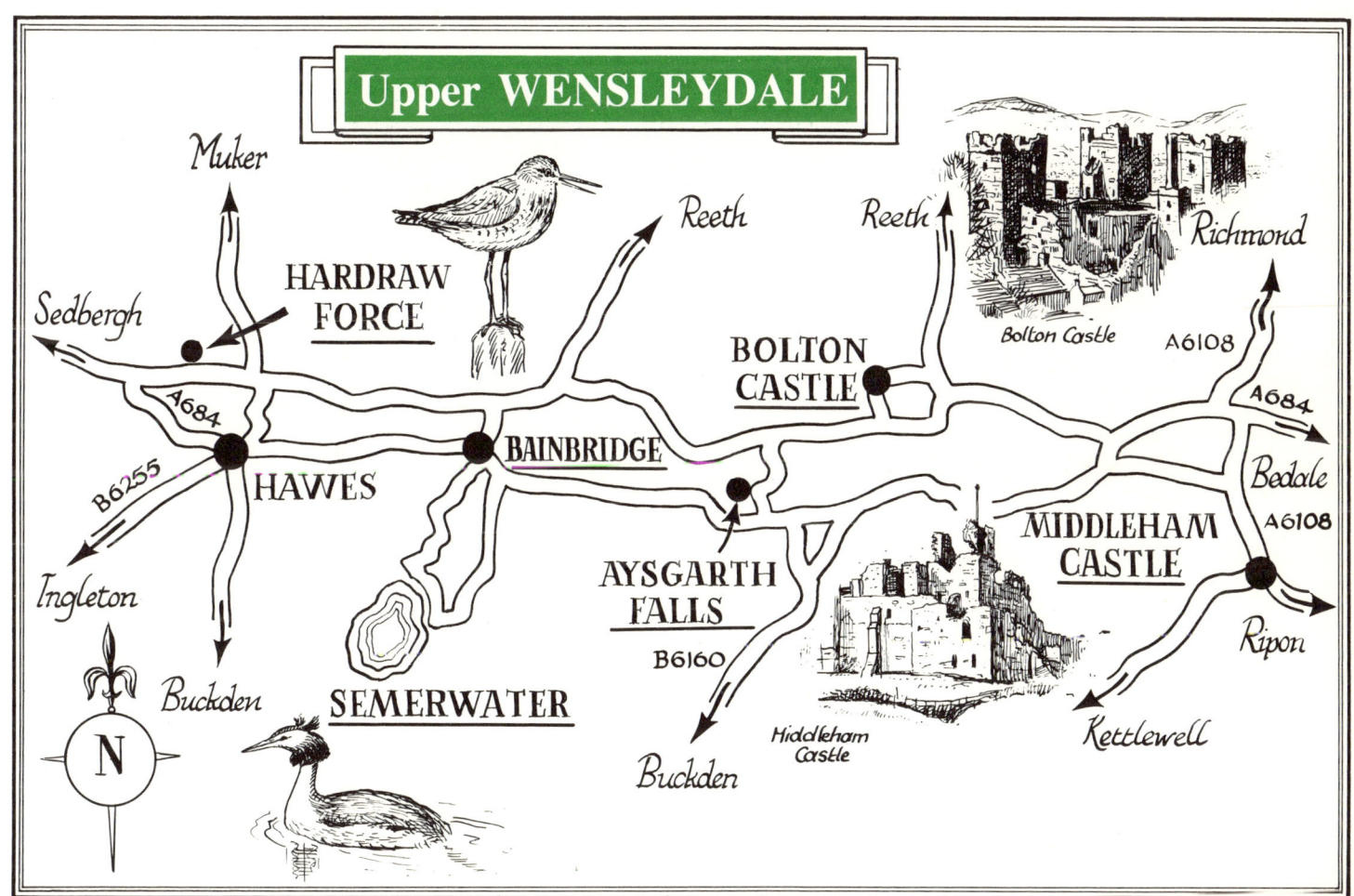

Upper WENSLEYDALE

Muker

Sedbergh

HARDRAW FORCE

A684

B6255

HAWES

Ingleton

Buckden

N

SEMERWATER

BAINBRIDGE

Reeth

BOLTON CASTLE

Reeth

Richmond

Bolton Castle

A6108

A684

Bedale

A6108

MIDDLEHAM CASTLE

AYSGARTH FALLS

B6160

Middleham Castle

Buckden

Ripon

Kettlewell

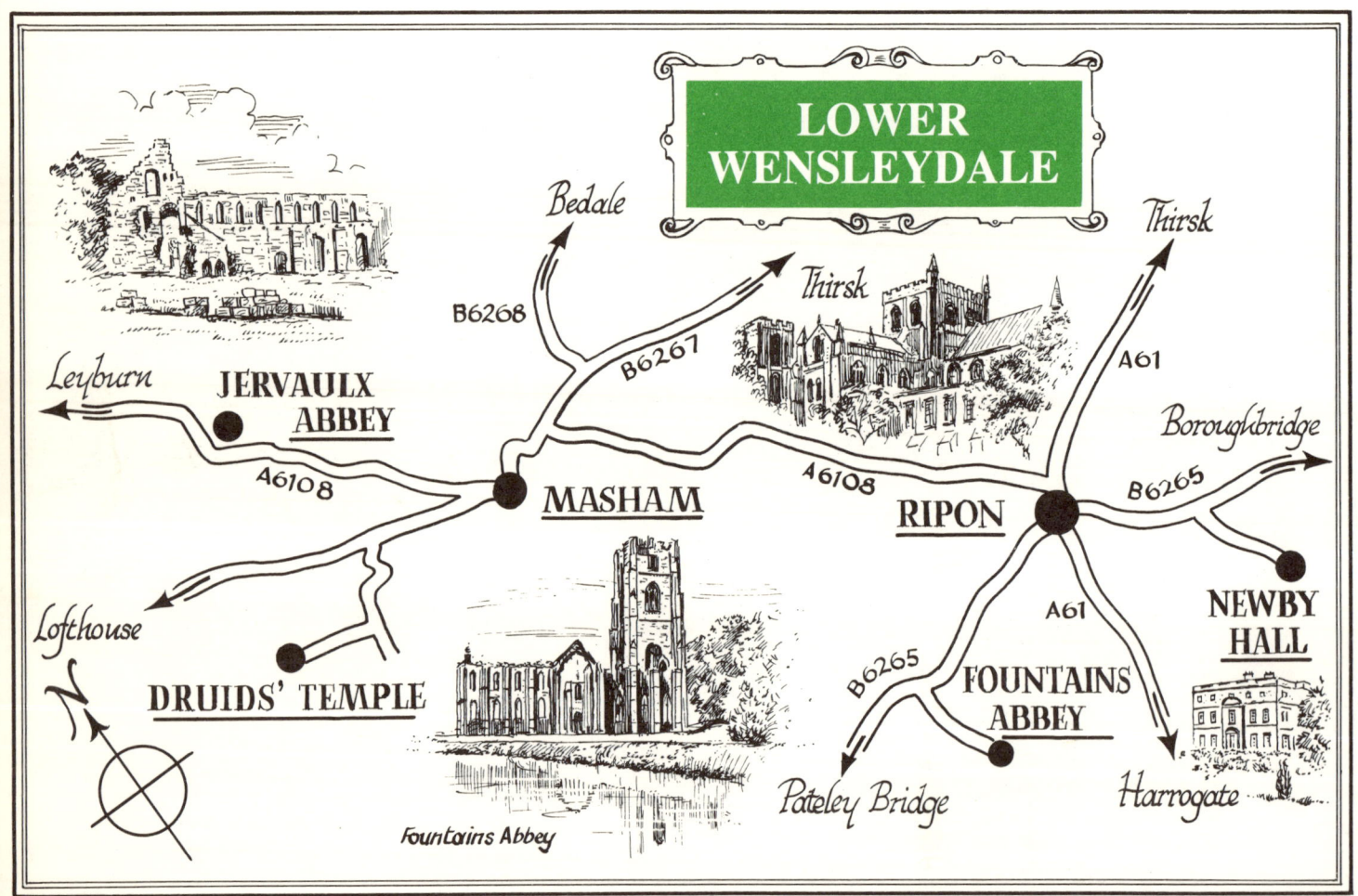

LOWER WENSLEYDALE

Leyburn

JERVAULX ABBEY

A6108

Lofthouse

DRUIDS' TEMPLE

N

Bedale

B6268

B6267

Thirsk

MASHAM

A6108

RIPON

Thirsk

A61

Boroughbridge

B6265

NEWBY HALL

A61

B6265

FOUNTAINS ABBEY

Pateley Bridge

Harrogate

Fountains Abbey

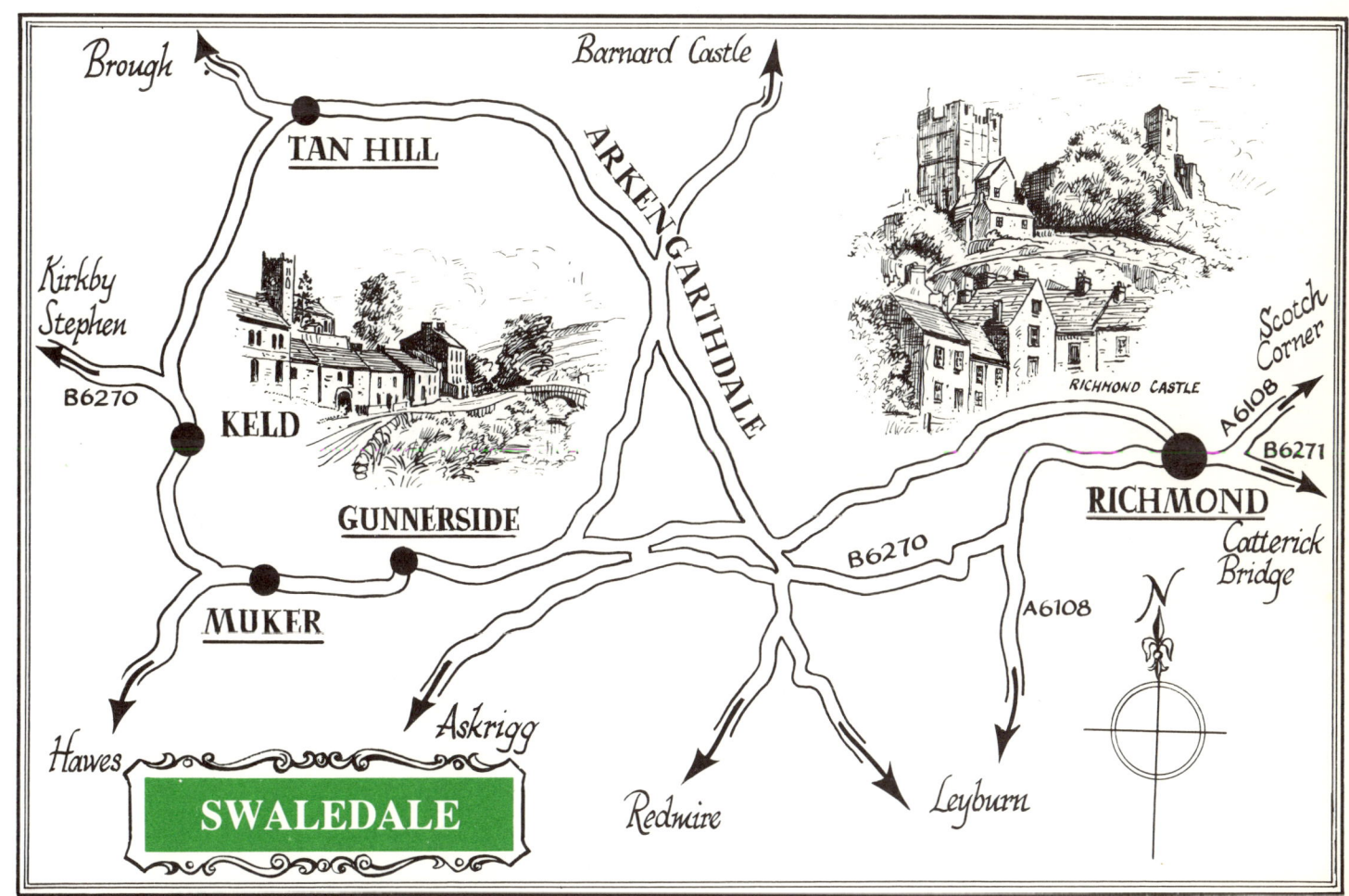

Brough

TAN HILL

Barnard Castle

ARKENGARTHDALE

Kirkby
Stephen

B6270

KELD

GUNNERSIDE

MUKER

Hawes

Askrigg

SWALEDALE

Redmire

B6270

A6108

Leyburn

RICHMOND CASTLE

RICHMOND

Scotch
Corner

A6108

B6271

Catterick
Bridge

N